Never Give Up on your Dreams

Never Give Up on your Dreams
"Finding the strength to get up again"

Written by:
PuleSir
Author | Agent of Change | Inspirational Speaker
"Inspiring people to live their lives to the fullest."

Book Artwork and Formatting by PuleSir
Email: itpule@gmail.com
Twitter: @PuleSir
Facebook: @PuleSir
Instagram: @PuleSir
LinkedIn: @PuleSir

Copyright © 2021 PuleSir

All rights reserved.

No part of this book may be reproduced, stored in a retrieval system, or transmitted in any form or by any means—electronic, mechanical, photocopying, recording, scanning, or otherwise—without the prior written permission of the publisher.

ISBN: 978-0-620-96754-9

Contents

Introduction 7

1. Understand the importance of having dreams 13
2. Understand the importance of achieving your dreams 41
3. Protect your dreams against dream killers 53
4. Overcome the unexpected and discouragement . 93
5. Don't lose hope, and don't give up 107
6. It is not over with you. Don't give up 121
7. The ingredients to achieve your dreams 147

Dreams do come true 177
About the Author 179

Introduction

"Nowhere in your life were you told that life would be smooth without obstacles. As such, don't expect it to be." **- PuleSir**

God blessed us with a precious gift we call **life,** to live and enjoy it to the fullest. He also blessed us with gifts, skills, ideas, and creative minds to help us be successful and significant. He created us to be the best and live the lives we desire to live to the fullest.

We have dreams that we want to achieve. Dreams that we know or believe can transform our lives positively. We also have ideas that if we can make them a reality, our lives will improve.

But sometimes, the unexpected takes place in our lives, and instead of achieving our dreams, we face obstacles and countless problems challenging us and sometimes tearing us apart. They cause us to fail many times and fall so badly. And because of this, we lose interest in our lives, leading us to see no purpose in living or pursuing our dreams.

Unfortunately, that is where most people lose it all and give up in life. They find themselves no longer interested in anything or no longer excited about their dreams or the future they were looking forward to. They end up settling for anything that comes their way.

"Don't be one of them. And if you already are, I want you to find the strength to get up again. Dream again. Be excited again about life and the future you want to have. It is possible and achievable."

The truth is that regardless of who you are or where you come from, you will come across challenges and face the unexpected in life. They will hurt you, disappoint you, break you down, and push you hard to the ground. *But that's part of life, not the end of it.*

I want you to know and understand that even if you have challenges and problems in every corner of your life, they are not meant to break you but to build and help you grow stronger.

"You don't grow when life is going easy for you, but when faced with life's challenges."

Through hardships, you can unleash your true potential and your inner strength. Through tough times, you can learn more about yourself and be refined to be the best you are born to be.

Never let anything stop you from achieving your dreams and living your life to the fullest. Never allow anything to limit you or cause you to settle for anything less than what you should have or achieve.

"Focus and never allow anything to shift your focus on your dreams and the life you desire to live. Challenges will always be there, but never allow them to shift your focus." - **PuleSir.**

The main goal of this book is to help you realise how important it is for you to have dreams and make them a reality. I want you also to be able to protect your dreams against dream killers so that dream killers will not kill your dreams, but you will achieve them.

You will also learn how to overcome the unexpected and discouragement you will face as you pursue your dreams. And the last chapter will bless you with the ingredients you need to mix to achieve your dreams.

If you have already given up on your dreams or are no longer excited about them, this book will help you to dream again and be excited again about living your life to the fullest. You will stay determined and never allow anything to discourage you or deny you the opportunity to be the best that God created you to be.

"Your dreams can change your life positively if you achieve them and not give up on them."

Introduction

As you read this book, remember that *"Dreams do come true."* No matter how big they are, how long it takes, and the challenges you face or how often you fall or fail as you pursue those dreams. Therefore, **"Never Give Up on your Dreams."**

Chapter 1

Understand the importance of having dreams

"Dreams do come true, vision can be a reality, and success is possible and achievable." **- PuleSir**

Have you ever wondered why some people have dreams, achieve them, and live their lives to the fullest, while others have dreams but never achieve those dreams?

Have you ever wondered why some people succeed or live their lives to the fullest while others settle for anything that comes their way or struggle in life?

In most cases, those who you see having dreams, achieving them, succeeding in life, or living their lives to the fullest understand the importance of having dreams and what achieving their dreams can do to their lives or the impact that dreams can have in their lives.

That is why they don't give up when they face challenges and don't allow anything to stop them from achieving their dreams.

But most people who settle for anything that comes their way or settle for a mediocre life don't understand the importance of having dreams, don't have dreams, or don't care about having dreams and the difference dreams can make in their lives.

Others had dreams but gave up on them when they faced challenges. Instead of facing and overcoming those challenges, they gave up, allowing those challenges to stop them from dreaming or achieving their dreams.

That is why you need to understand the importance of having dreams. And the importance of achieving those dreams so that you will not settle for a mediocre life or anything that comes your way. And you will not keep wondering why others are succeeding while you are not or why others have dreams and achieve them while you don't.

If you can understand the importance of having dreams, you will realise the need to have your own dreams. You will also understand the need to plan and take action to achieve those dreams so that you can live and enjoy your life to the fullest. You will be part of those people who had dreams and achieved them, not those who never had dreams or who had dreams but never achieved them.

If you can understand the importance of having dreams, nothing will stop you from pursuing and achieving your dreams and being the best you are born to be. Nothing will prevent you from living the life you desire to live to the fullest. *You will be unstoppable and successful.*

You will find inspiration to dream big and refuse to let anything hold you back or prevent you from achieving your dreams. You will not wish for what others have, but you will know what you want, pursue it, and achieve it.

If you can understand the importance of having dreams, you will be encouraged to dream big. You will be excited about having dreams and never allow anybody to tell you that your dreams are impossible to achieve or will not come true. You will no longer entertain negative thoughts and negative people who are always crushing and opposing your ideas and plans.

Instead of being discouraged by the negativity around you, it will inspire you to pursue and achieve your dreams. It will encourage you to go all out and make sure that you live your life to the fullest.

I believe one of the reasons you purchased this book and are reading it is that you don't want to give up on your dreams but to achieve them. Or you want to know how you can achieve your dreams and find the inspiration to keep you motivated to achieve them and live your life to the fullest. *Be assured that you will find all that in this book.*

Why is it important to have dreams?

Dreams can give you the life you desire to live. They can give you the desires of your heart and open doors of success for you. They can take you from being nobody to being somebody. They can connect you with your destiny helpers or relevant people who will help you to be the best or be who God created you to be. *That is how powerful dreams are and why you need to have them.*

Dreams give you hope. Without dreams, you feel hopeless and defeated. You feel stuck, and chances for you to give up on yourself and in life are very high. But when you have dreams, you have hope that things will not remain the same. You have hope that your life can turn around positively through your dreams. And you somehow find the strength and courage to keep going forward no matter what you face.

Dreams give you purpose. Without dreams, you become nobody. Without dreams, you go nowhere. Without dreams, you aim for nothing, and you achieve nothing. Without dreams, you have no direction. Without dreams, you don't have a purpose, and you end up living and dying without accomplishing anything or making any change in this world.

But when you have dreams, you become clear about what you want and where you are going. You become inspired to keep going forward. No matter how many times you fall or how many challenges you face.

Dreams can solve your problems. They inspire and cause you to think beyond what you see or are going through. They expand your imagination. For example, if you are struggling financially, having a dream to be financially able and stable can cause or inspire you to think beyond that situation. It can help you envision yourself as financially secure and stable.

That dream will inspire you to plan and take action to move from struggling financially to being financially able and stable. You will start thinking and producing ideas to generate income and solve your financial problems.

You won't allow that financial struggle to defeat or define you, but you will overcome it through your dreams. *That is how powerful dreams are or can be and why you need to have them.*

Dreams are change makers; they bring change. People who contributed positively to this world and made changes had dreams and understood the importance of having those dreams. Hence, they achieved them.

For example, we use smartphones and laptops, drive different cars, and have a variety of furniture in our homes. We see change in our society, and all that is because someone had a dream and understood the importance of having that dream. They pursued it, made sure it became true, and produced results.

Had it not been for someone having a dream and achieving it, we would not be seeing the changes or inventions happening around us.

Yes, they faced challenges. They failed many times. They were criticised and mocked. They got tired, and others thought they were crazy, but they overcame all that because they believed and focused on their dreams.

They understood the importance of having those dreams and believed that dreams do come true. *And guess what? Their dreams came true.*

Through your dreams, you can make the change you want to see in your life, family, community, or wherever you see the need for a change.

Dreams are a vision of the life you want or things you can do and have. From where you are, you can see where you can be or want to be in years to come. Your dreams answer, *"Where do you see yourself 5, 10, 20 years from now?"* And not only do they answer that question, but they also help you get there.

Dreams help you see the future you want and how to get there. They inspire you to have a better life or the life of your dreams. Dreams direct your life, taking you from nowhere to somewhere.

Dreams are your guideline, guiding you on how to live your life. They help you develop your character and know how to behave and live well with others. They can guide you in choosing who to associate with and who not to associate with. They can also help you understand which places to hang around and which ones to avoid or not to hang around.

They guide your decision-making and can help you to be a disciplined person. Ultimately, your dreams can make your life easier to live and enjoy.

Dreams serve as the inspiration you need to wake up in the morning. If you have dreams, you don't need an alarm to wake you up. They excite you and give you a reason to live. They inspire you to wake up in the morning, no matter how things are in your life. When you remember them, something inside you pushes you to wake up and face a new day with a positive and winning attitude.

The Power of Your Dreams

When I think of how powerful dreams are, I remember **Proverbs 18:16,** *"A man's gift makes room for him and brings him before great men."* The other version says, *"A man's gift opens doors*

That is how powerful your gift is. And *how powerful your dream can be.* For example, if you dream of writing a book and being an author, that book can open doors of success for you and bring you before great men.

If you dream of starting a business, that dream can open doors of success for you. Through achieving that dream, you can meet great people who can inspire you to dream more and be a better person. You can generate income that will sustain you and your family.

Whatever dream you have, if you pursue and achieve it, it will open doors of success for you and bring you before great men. *That is the power of a dream.*

If I did not have a dream, you would not be reading this book today, and even if I had a dream but gave up on it, you would not be reading my book. But since you are reading it, it proves that *dreams do come true.*

It proves that I had a dream to write a book and achieved it. It is proof that you can have dreams and achieve them. Finally, it proves that you can achieve your dreams if you plan and take action.

It is important for you to have dreams. And it is also important to understand the importance of having those dreams. If you can get that right, you will be unstoppable, and none of your dreams will be left unattended or not achieved.

Understanding the importance of having dreams will help you to have your own dreams, achieve them, and live your life to the fullest.

"Your dreams will open doors of success for you and give you the life you desire to live."

Be clear about your reasons for pursuing your dreams

As much as it is important to have dreams, it is also important to be clear about the reasons behind those dreams.

- Do you have that dream because your friend had it and achieved it?
- Do you have that dream because your colleague had it and achieved it?
- Do you have that dream because your relative had it and achieved it?
- Do you have that dream because you are competing with others?
- Do you have that dream because you heard someone talking about it and the difference achieving it can make in one's life, and suddenly you made it yours?

What are your reasons for having that dream or to want to achieve it?

If your reasons are wrong, chances are that you will not achieve it, and if you can achieve it, chances are that you will not enjoy the results because your reasons were wrong. You will not be as excited and proud of yourself as the person who had good reasons to pursue that same dream will be.

If you have that dream because you are competing with your friend, colleague, or relative, chances are you will not achieve it. You will end up confused and no longer clear or sure about where you are going or what you want to achieve.

I have seen that happening a lot, and unfortunately, many lives have been destroyed because of that competition.

Jealousy is also a product of having a dream because you want to compete with others. You are forever jealous of them and can even develop hatred towards them. And as they continue to pursue and achieve their dreams, you get more confused, angry, and hate them. *That is unnecessary and can be very dangerous.*

I have seen people register to study a particular course because their friends, colleagues, or relatives are studying it or are qualified in that field of study. Unfortunately, because it was not their dream, they never achieved it.

I have seen people start businesses because their friends, colleagues, or relatives have businesses. But because it was not their dream, they did not achieve it.

The wrong reasons behind having your dream will forever disappoint you. And if you are not careful, you will be jealous and envy other people's dreams or successes. And you will be full of hatred towards people who achieve their dreams and live their lives to the fullest. You will forever compete with others.

If your reasons are wrong, you will give up easily. Nothing will encourage you, and you will end up asking yourself, *"What is the point of having this dream, or why am I pursuing it?"* That is when you will give up because it is not worth pursuing a dream that is not yours.

You don't know why your friend, colleague, or relative had that dream. Hence, they persevered, and you cannot.

You need to have an honest conversation with yourself and be clear about your reasons for having your dreams. Stop having dreams because others had them and achieved them.

Stop having dreams because you want to compete with others. You will fail and find yourself frustrated and bitter. You will find yourself confused and angry with everyone, even with people who are supposed to help you succeed in life.

Understand the purpose of your dreams

If I did not understand the purpose of my dreams and the importance of having them, and if I did not believe in my dreams and myself to achieve them, *I would not have written this book, and you would not be reading it today.*

But because I had a dream to encourage you to live your life to the fullest, a dream to write a book that will inspire you to never give up on your dreams, and I clearly understood the purpose of that dream, I achieved it. And here you are, reading that book—the book I wanted to write for you, and I believe it will definitely inspire you to *never give up on your dreams.*

Whenever I felt discouraged to continue writing this book, I reminded myself why I was writing it, and that kept me going and encouraged me. Whenever negative thoughts overwhelmed me, I remembered the purpose of writing this book, and I overcame a lot of negative thoughts and the distractions I encountered.

Whenever fear and doubt tried to intimidate me, telling me that I was not good enough to write this book and no one would purchase and read it, I remembered the purpose of writing it, and guess what? I achieved that dream, and you are reading that book.

> *"You need to understand the purpose of your dreams and reasons why you have those dreams."*

If your dream is to be an author like me, *"What is the purpose of that dream?"* If your dream is to be wealthy or to be financially able and stable, *"What is the purpose of that dream?"*

Maybe you want to be a doctor, nurse, inspirational speaker, teacher, politician, etc. *What is the purpose of that dream? What are your reasons for having that dream? Why do you want to achieve it, or why is it important to you?*

If you don't understand or don't have a purpose for your dreams, and if your reasons for having those dreams are wrong, you will be easily discouraged and irritated and might never achieve them.

People who understand the importance of having dreams also understand the purpose of having those dreams. They know their *why*, and that is the reason they can have dreams and achieve them.

Have good reasons

Good reasons behind your dreams will help you have a better life. However, wrong reasons or reasons driven by unhealthy motivations, such as competition with others, can have a negative impact on your life. It is, therefore, necessary to have good intentions or reasons why you have those dreams and want to achieve them.

You have to be able to ask yourself, *"Why is this dream important to me? Why do I want to achieve it, and what is its purpose?"* Be able to answer those questions because if you cannot, you will struggle to achieve your dreams.

Be clear about your reasons for pursuing your dreams, and make sure they are the right reasons to keep you inspired to achieve your dreams.

Your *"Why you have that dream"* is very important because it can build or break you. If it is for the wrong reasons, it can leave you discouraged. But if it is for good reasons, it can keep you going when you face challenges and inspire you when you feel discouraged or surrounded by negativity.

That is why it is important to be clear on why you pursue that dream and keep reminding yourself of that.

Believe in your dreams and in yourself to achieve them

Eleanor Roosevelt said, *"The future belongs to those who believe in the beauty of their dreams."* And she got it right because it is not enough to have dreams. You have to believe in them and believe that they can come true. You have to believe that they can make a difference in your life and give you the future you want to have. *Believe in the beauty of your dreams.*

You also have to believe in yourself and that you have what it takes to have dreams and to achieve them. Believe that you can face and overcome any challenge you will encounter while pursuing your dreams. If you don't believe in yourself to achieve your dreams, you will give up easily and never achieve those dreams.

Believing in your dreams and yourself to achieve them gives you the strength and courage you need to make your dreams come true. It helps you overcome negativity, no matter where it comes from or how strong it might be. You can overcome anything that wants to come between you and achieving your dreams.

Believing in your dreams and yourself to achieve them will help you overcome the doubt, fear, and discouragement we often encounter when pursuing our dreams. When someone says to you, *"It is impossible for you to achieve this dream,"* you will be able to respond confidently to them and say, *"Nothing is impossible for me to achieve."*

When no one believes in your dreams or that you can achieve them, you will not be stressed or discouraged because you will be the one who believes in your dreams and yourself to achieve them. When doubt and fear try to intimidate or discourage you, they will not succeed. You will face and overcome them. *You will be unstoppable.*

You are reading this book because I had a dream to become an author and write books that inspire people worldwide. I believed in that dream and in myself to achieve it, and for you to read this book today is proof that my dream came true.

It is proof that I believed in my dream, and I believed in myself to achieve that dream, and I achieved it. I faced doubt, fear, negativity, and all that tried to intimidate and stop me. But none of that succeeded because I believed in my dream and in myself to achieve it, no matter what.

"Believe that you can achieve your dreams, and they can make a difference in your life."

The difference your dreams can make in your life

Your dreams can have a significant impact on your life. They have the power to shape your thoughts, emotions, and actions and can even influence the course of your life. Dreams can inspire you to set goals and motivate you to plan and take action to achieve those goals. They can give you a sense of purpose and direction.

Dreams have the unimaginable power to inspire and help you overcome challenges and obstacles. They can provide hope and confidence in yourself and the future you are looking forward to.

Whether you are pursuing a personal or professional goal, your dreams can be a powerful force that drives you forward and helps you achieve your full potential.

Understanding the importance of having dreams will be the encouragement, guidance, and inspiration you need to achieve your dreams and live your life to the fullest.

Believing in your dreams and in yourself to achieve them will help you overcome whatever challenge you will face while pursuing those dreams. You will not be intimidated by doubt and fear.

Being clear about your reasons for having your dreams and understanding their purpose will help you persevere. You will never give up on your dreams; you will achieve them and enjoy your life to the fullest.

That clearness will also prevent you from competing with others or being jealous when they succeed or achieve their dreams. You will stay in your lane and be proud of your progress and achievements.

Knowing the difference your dreams can make in your life will boost your confidence, develop a hunger for success, and inspire you to keep going no matter what you face while pursuing your dreams.

"Understanding the importance of having dreams will help you to have dreams and achieve them."

I believe, by now, you understand why it is important for you to have dreams and why you must have good reasons for having those dreams.

I believe you also understand the difference dreams can make in your life and why you must believe in your dreams and in yourself to achieve those dreams.

Hopefully, you are now excited and encouraged to have dreams and make a difference in your life and the lives of those looking up to you.

But remember that *having dreams is not enough.* You have to achieve those dreams. After all, what is the point of having dreams if you are not going to achieve them? How will they make a difference in your life if you don't achieve them? *More on this in the next Chapter.*

Chapter 2

Understand the importance of achieving your dreams

"Your dreams are waiting for you to plan and take action to achieve them, so that they can give you the life you desire to live." - **PuleSir**

What is the point of having dreams if you are not going to achieve them? What is the purpose of dreaming big if you are not going to make those dreams come true? What is the use of having dreams if you don't intend to plan and take action to achieve them?

Remember, no matter how great your dreams are and regardless of the difference they can make in your life, *if you don't achieve them, they will remain as dreams.* And they will make no difference or have no impact on your life.

Sadly, if you don't achieve your dreams, your life will remain the same, and you will be worse than someone who never had dreams because your dreams will turn into nightmares that will keep you awake at night.

You will live a life full of regrets simply because you had great dreams but never achieved them. Dreams that you know could have impacted your life.

> *"It is important to have dreams, but it is also important to achieve those dreams."*

Why is it important for you to achieve your dreams?

Dreams can give you the life you desire to live. They can make a difference in your life by turning bad situations into good ones. They can turn your life around positively, taking you from where you are to where you want to be.

Through pursuing and achieving your dreams, you can unleash your true potential and set yourself up for a successful and rewarding future. You can get out of your comfort zone and be a better person.

Achieving your dreams can bring happiness and a sense of purpose or fulfilment. It can make your life meaningful and worth living. You will live your life to the fullest with fewer or no regrets. And because of your achievements, you will be happy and proud of yourself.

Achieving your dreams can inspire others. Some will come to you and ask for your advice. They will want to know how you made it to where you are or how you achieved your dreams. You will be able to inspire and guide them to pursue their own dreams and to achieve them.

Achieving your dreams is a completion of what you started. It is proof that you can have dreams and achieve them. It gives you the results of what you have been planting and takes you from where you are to where you want to be.

Achieving your dreams will increase your motivation and the drive to dream more. It will boost and improve your confidence and self-esteem. It can open doors of success for you and bring you before great men and women who will inspire and help you to live your life to the fullest. *But that can only happen if you have dreams and achieve them.*

On the other hand, failing to achieve your dreams or accomplish what you truly desire can negatively impact your life. It may result in settling for less than you deserve and missing out on significant opportunities that could have improved your life. Again, not achieving your dreams can lead to feelings of regret, dissatisfaction, and a sense of purposelessness.

For example, let us say you take a step back and examine your life. And you notice the financial struggle and poverty your family is experiencing.

To overcome this, you dream of attending school and pursuing a specific course that will lead you to a higher-paying job or running your company. By doing so, you can provide for your family and lift them out of the financial struggle they are currently facing.

If you achieve that dream, you will be able to defeat poverty and the financial struggle experienced by your family. You will also inspire them, as you will be able to identify problems and solve them. Your success will also inspire others, showing them that they can have dreams and achieve them. In essence, achieving your dreams can be a life-changing solution that can give you the life you desire and deserve.

However, if you fail to achieve that dream, your situation will remain unchanged and become worse. You and your family will continue to experience financial struggle and poverty. You will feel hopeless and defeated, believing that you are a failure because you failed to achieve your dream and get yourself and your family out of poverty.

That is why you must pursue and achieve your dreams, no matter how challenging the journey may seem. Dreams can help you solve your problems and get you out of the difficult situations you find yourself in. *They are the key to unlocking a better future.*

What causes people to have dreams but never achieve them?

There are several reasons why some people have dreams but never achieve them. One of the most common reasons is a lack of clarity about their dreams. When people don't have a clear idea of what they want to achieve, it becomes difficult to take the necessary steps towards achieving their dreams.

Another reason people don't achieve their dreams is their failure to take action. People who are not proactive in pursuing their dreams usually find themselves stuck in a rut and unable to make significant progress. *You cannot achieve your dreams if you don't plan and take action.*

Fear of failure or stepping outside their comfort zone is also a common reason why most people don't achieve their dreams. When individuals fear the possibility of failure or are doubtful about taking risks, they tend to avoid taking the necessary steps towards their dreams.

A lack of understanding about the importance of having and achieving their dreams can also be a roadblock. People who don't fully understand the value of their dreams may not have the motivation or drive to pursue them.

Confusing motives or having the wrong reasons for pursuing their dreams can also derail them from making their dreams come true. When individuals have misguided or unclear reasons for pursuing their dreams, they may lack the passion and commitment to make their dreams come true.

Some people had great dreams but did not achieve them because of dream killers. Dream killers killed their dreams before they could achieve them. They let their negative thoughts, people, and circumstances destroy their dreams.

Unfortunately, they never achieved the great dreams they had.

These are some common reasons why people have dreams but fail to achieve them. However, you don't have to be one of them. You can do things differently by being clear about what you want. You can plan and take action to achieve your dreams.

Don't let fear of failure keep you from taking risks or trying new things. Be clear about why you have dreams, and understand the importance of achieving them.

Understanding the importance of achieving your dreams will inspire you to wake up every day and make your dreams come true. It will help you stay motivated and focused on your path to success. You will not give up until you achieve your dreams.

It is, therefore, important to be specific about what you want in life and define your dreams accordingly. Once you have a clear picture of your dreams, you can create a plan and take action towards making them a reality.

Always remember that the journey towards achieving your dreams may be challenging, and you may encounter obstacles. However, with determination, perseverance, and a positive attitude, you can overcome those challenges and ultimately turn your dreams into a reality.

> *"No matter how great your dreams are and regardless of the impact they can make in your life, if you don't achieve those dreams, they will make no difference in your life."*
> **- PuleSir**

Please don't add to the list of people who had great dreams but never achieved them—people whose lives are full of regrets because they had dreams that could have made a difference in their lives. Unfortunately, they failed to achieve those dreams. *Make sure you achieve your dreams.*

Always remember to protect your dreams from dream killers, no matter how great they are. Dream killers are people or circumstances that can destroy your dreams. Therefore, it is critical to safeguard your dreams against such individuals or situations. Otherwise, you will have dreams but never achieve them. *We will discuss this topic in more detail in the next chapter.*

Chapter 3

Protect your dreams against dream killers

"Dream killers will always be there, wanting to kill your dreams. But never allow them to succeed." - **PuleSir**

Dream killers can have a negative impact on your life. Not only can they destroy your dreams and your life, but they can also destroy the lives of those who would have benefited from your dreams. *Can you imagine that? The damage caused by dream killers.*

They can cause you to lose hope, motivation, and confidence, which can have long-lasting and far-reaching effects on your life. They can instantly destroy the dreams you have nurtured and worked towards, leaving you feeling lost and confused.

It is painful to have a conversation with someone who had a dream but never achieved it. You can feel the pain and regret in their voice. Sometimes, tears will roll down their face while talking to you, simply because of where they are instead of where they should be had they achieved their dreams.

They failed to protect their dreams against dream killers. And unfortunately, dream killers killed their dreams. *Please don't add to that list, but be aware of dream killers and protect your dreams against them.*

What are dream killers?

Dream killers are enemies of your success. They are the things that want to keep you where you are and never achieve your dreams. It can be anyone or anything that stands in the way of achieving your dreams and goals.

They can be external factors, such as negative people or a lack of resources or opportunities. Or they can be internal factors, such as self-doubt, comfort zone, laziness, or fear.

Negative people can undermine your confidence and discourage you from pursuing your dreams by criticising or belittling them. A lack of resources or opportunities can limit your ability to pursue your dreams.

Self-doubt and fear can prevent you from taking risks and stepping out of your comfort zone to achieve your dreams and goals.

Being aware and understanding dream killers and striving to overcome them can help you maintain motivation and focus on achieving your dreams.

Here is a list of dream killers to be aware of and protect your dreams against.

1. *Friends*

Your friends can kill your dreams. They can belittle you to the point where you completely doubt yourself and feel like you are nobody. They can instil fear in you and discourage you instead of encouraging you. *I wonder if we should really call such people friends or if we should call them wolves in sheep's clothing.*

It is a common experience that when you share your dreams with your friends, they may not take them seriously or even discourage you by saying things like *"Not you, my friend,"* or *"That is too ambitious for you."* These words can negatively impact your confidence and make you doubt yourself and your abilities.

There are those friends who, instead of being happy for you or excited about your dreams, will rather tell you all the reasons why you cannot achieve your dreams.

It is sad when you come across someone who had great dreams but did not achieve them. When you ask them what happened, they tell you *it is because of their friends* who never believed in them or believed they were capable of achieving anything.

Friends who were jealous to see their friend having dreams, achieving them, and living a better life. Sadly, they discouraged that person, and they never achieved the dreams they had.

Be bold enough to confront your friends.

When you share your dream with your friends, and they laugh at you, be bold enough to ask them why they are laughing at you. Ask them if it is because they don't see how you can have and achieve such a dream or what makes them laugh at you.

When you share your dream with your friends, and they start saying things like, *"Not you, my friend, stop being crazy, etc."* Be bold enough to ask them why they are saying that. *Why not you?* Don't just agree with their negativity and kill your dreams, but stand up for what you believe in.

It is important to surround yourself with supportive friends who believe in your potential and offer encouragement and motivation to help you achieve your dreams, not friends who will kill them. Don't let anyone's words or opinions hold you back from pursuing your dreams and living your life to the fullest, no matter how close that person is to you.

If necessary, cut that friend out of your life instead of not achieving your dreams because of them. After all, what is the point of having people in your life who discourage you and don't believe in you and your dreams?

If someone discourages you from pursuing or achieving your dreams, that person is destroying your life and the future you could have. *Please protect your dreams against such people.*

2. *Parents*

As much as we believe or expect our parents to support and encourage us to have dreams or be excited about our dreams, they can be dream killers and kill our dreams.

There are parents who, instead of encouraging and supporting their children to pursue and achieve their dreams, will instead want to achieve their dreams through their children. They want to live their lives or the lives they could not live through their children.

Such an instance is when, as a child, you dream of becoming a teacher, but your father wants you to play soccer because that is the dream he had and could not achieve. He will buy soccer boots for you or all you need to play soccer because he wants you to be the soccer star he dreamed of becoming.

He will not even pay attention to your dream of becoming a teacher. He will instead crush it and encourage you to play soccer. *That is a dream killer—your parent killing your dream.*

Sometimes, when you share your dreams with your parents, they may not understand or support you. Instead of offering encouragement and support, they may react with disbelief or ridicule. And ask you questions like, *"Who have you seen achieving that dream? What makes you think you can achieve that dream? Why don't you study a particular course, find a job, and stop with those dreams of yours?"*

That is painful, especially coming from your parents, whom you believed would be excited and supportive.

Some parents kill their children's dreams because of competition with other parents. When your parents use you to compete with other parents instead of them supporting you to be who you are born to be or dream to be. Such an instance is when they want you to follow dreams that they believe will make them look like great parents who raised wonderful and successful children.

When you tell your parents that your dream is to be something or achieve something they look down on or don't consider significant, they crush that dream and force you to do something else or study a course they can brag about to other parents. They don't realise or maybe don't care that what they are doing is killing your dreams.

Some parents kill their children's dreams because they want them to follow in their footsteps. If your mother has been successful as a teacher or a singer, she may want you to pursue the same path. They saw it working for them and believe it will also work for you. And they do that without asking or considering what your dream could be.

There is nothing wrong with being inspired by your parent's dream or chosen career and wanting to follow it. We have seen that happening a lot. Where a son became a soccer star like his father and a daughter became a singer like her mother or father. There is nothing wrong with that. *But it has to be something you, as a child, dream of or want to do.*

After all, God placed different dreams in us for a purpose. If he gave you a dream similar to your parents', pursue it. But if you are doing it because your parents are forcing you to, then they are killing the one you are born to pursue and fulfil.

It is discouraging and painful to have your dreams killed by your parents. You become discouraged and angry. And you will even ask yourself why God gave you such parents who are not supportive.

If that's the case for you, talk to your parents and make them understand why you have those dreams and the difference achieving them will make in your lives. Let them know why those dreams are important to you. And why you have to pursue and achieve them.

Make them aware that you understand that they care about you. And you are not at any point disrespecting them or their decisions, but you want to do something you are passionate about. They might change and support you or remain to say, *"They know what is good for you."* But don't let them kill your dreams.

It is necessary to remember that everyone has a unique path in life, and it is up to you to pursue your dreams even if your parents are not supporting you. Find people who will support and encourage you to pursue and achieve your dreams. *You are not being disrespectful; you are pursuing what God placed in your heart to fulfil what He created you for.*

3. *Your Partner*

Remember that not everyone will be excited about your dreams or support you in achieving them. That includes your partner. At times, they will not be as excited as you are about your dreams, and others will discourage you and tell you all the reasons why you should forget about pursuing those dreams. *Your partner can kill your dreams.*

It is painful to have someone in your life who does not believe in you or your dreams, especially when achieving those dreams will benefit that person. If you achieve your dreams, your partner's life will improve, and your relationship will be more enjoyable.

For example, if you dream of starting a business to generate or increase your income, surely achieving that dream will help you take care of your partner or assist them financially. Your family will not struggle financially.

But, sadly, not all partners see it that way. You will have a partner who will crush your ideas or your dreams. And this is because what you saw is not what they are seeing, or what God placed in your heart is not what He placed in their hearts.

Others will say they do it out of love and protecting you from disappointments or being hurt. But they don't realise that they are the ones disappointing and hurting you by doubting you, not believing in you, not believing in your dreams, and crushing those dreams. They don't realise that they are dream killers killing your dreams.

It is, therefore, important to know that your partner might not be as excited as you are about your dreams and might also not be as supportive as you want them to be. But don't allow that to discourage you, and don't let it kill your dreams. *Pursue your dreams and achieve them with or without your partner's support.*

4. *Your Colleagues*

Your colleagues can kill your dreams, especially if they don't have dreams or fail to see life beyond their workplace. Most of the time, they will be negative and discouraging.

When you share your dreams and plans with them, their response will often be discouraging. They will tell you why your plans might not work or question why you would risk your job with a dream you are not sure will come true. They will remind you of the salary you earn every month, the benefits you receive from the company, and everything that will cause you to question your decision.

If you are not careful or don't understand the importance of having your dreams, you will easily fall for what they say and give up on those dreams. They will instil fear in you and cause you to doubt your decision to pursue your dreams.

Be careful of your colleagues, especially those who don't want to see you grow or who lack dreams or vision outside of work. Their negative attitude and lack of inspiration can hinder your dreams and ambitions. *Their negativity can kill your dreams.*

5. *People who never achieved their dreams or who lost hope.*

It is often said that surrounding yourself with people who have achieved success and are positive can help you achieve your dreams. But it is equally necessary to be conscious of the impact that people who have never accomplished their dreams or have lost hope can have on you.

Others may not intentionally try to discourage you from pursuing your dreams. But their negative attitude and lack of ambition can rub off on you and kill your dreams.

On the other hand, some of those who never achieved their dreams will intentionally discourage you from pursuing yours. Whenever you share your dreams with them, they will do all they can to instil fear and doubt in you. They will tell you all the negative stories that will discourage you or even cause you to give up on your dreams. After all, that is their goal. They want you to be like them and never achieve your dreams.

Surround yourself with supportive, encouraging, and optimistic individuals who uplift you and help you stay motivated to pursue and achieve your dreams. Also, be careful who you share your dreams with. *Some people should only see the results, not your plans.*

6. *Pursuing your dream for the wrong reasons.*

Having the wrong reasons for pursuing your dreams can kill them. It can lead you to failure. Suppose your reasons are driven by external factors such as societal pressure, competition, or the need for approval from others rather than a true passion for the dream itself. In that case, it will be difficult for you to achieve that dream.

It is easy to give up when you have the wrong reasons. After all, you have nothing to encourage you, and you will soon tell yourself, *"This dream is not worth pursuing."* And just like that, you will give up pursuing it.

It is important to have the right reasons behind your dreams, as having the wrong reasons can ultimately lead to failure. When pursuing a dream, examine your intentions and make sure they align with your values and desires. *Doing that will give you the inspiration and determination to persist through the challenges and obstacles that come your way.*

7. Competing with others

Competing with others or comparing yourself to them can discourage you and kill your dreams. When you compete with others or compare your success to theirs, you might feel left behind or like you took the wrong route to success.

When your dreams take longer to come true, while those you are competing with are achieving their dreams, you will be discouraged. But if you are not competing with them or comparing your success to theirs, you will be encouraged by their success because you will know that if they can achieve their dreams, you too can achieve yours.

Be proud of your small steps and focus on your journey and the progress you are making, regardless of how it measures up to others. *Don't compare yourself with others because you will be discouraged.*

8. Proving a point or settling a score

I have realised that certain people start projects to prove a point or settle a score. For example, you will find someone who has been removed or fired from a particular project starting his own.

And not because it is something he is passionate about or interested in. But he will be doing it believing that he is proving a point to those who fired him that he can pursue that project and succeed with it without them.

But often, people who do that never succeed because they are pursuing someone's dream. They follow that dream out of anger and bitterness or to prove a point. Sadly, along the way they fail and let go of that dream.

Don't do that. Never pursue a dream that is not yours just because you want to prove a point. You want to prove others wrong or settle a score with them. *That is a total waste of time.*

It will delay you or shift your focus from your own dreams that you should pursue. After all, what will you gain from proving that point? Will your dreams be achieved, or will you have achieved someone else's dream?

9. Negative Words

The words we hear from others can impact our lives positively or negatively. When others speak negatively about our dreams, it can be destructive because negative words can plant seeds of doubt in our minds and make us question our abilities and dreams.

Those words can be from your parents, friends, teachers, or colleagues. Their negative words can kill your dreams.

Negative, discouraging, and painful words can hit you hard, leaving you discouraged and seeing no point in dreaming. And often, what makes matters worse is where those words come from because most of the time, they come from the people you thought would be on your side encouraging you.

But even if that is the case in your life, never let negative words kill your dreams, no matter who they come from.

Remind yourself why you have that dream and why it is important for you to achieve it. Your dreams are personal and unique. Never let someone else's negativity discourage you from pursuing them. *Instead, surround yourself with supportive and encouraging people who will lift and help you achieve your dreams.*

10.   *Your Job*

There is nothing wrong with looking for a job and working, especially when the goal is to earn money to pursue your dreams and have a better life. *But if you are not careful, working can kill your dreams.*

Some people started working because they needed the money to pursue their dreams. Be it to further their studies, refine their gifts, or start a business. Unfortunately, most of them ended up stuck with their jobs and no longer pursuing their dreams.

Some got comfortable and started enjoying the salary, house, car, and other benefits that the company offered them. They started eying for increases, bonuses, and promotions. And abandoned or forgot their dreams.

Others ended up in debt, making it difficult for them to save for their studies or business as planned. *That is what killed most people's dreams.* They started working with good intentions but ended up abandoning their dreams and no longer pursuing them.

It is understandable that sometimes, your job will be demanding and make it difficult for you to pursue your dreams. You will wake up very early, have hectic days at work, and when you come home, you are tired. *All you want to do is to take a bath, eat, and sleep.*

But unfortunately, *waking up, going to work, coming home, and sleeping* will kill your dreams. You need to find a way to do your job successfully and still pursue your dreams. You might need to wake up earlier than you used to or sleep late so that you can work on your dreams.

Success does not come easy. You have to work and sacrifice where needed. Do what you have to do so that you can achieve your dreams and have the things you want to have.

Let your job sponsor your dreams and not kill them. It takes time. It is not easy, but it is possible. Don't be comfortable with your salary or company's benefits, and forget about your dreams. *Don't forget why you are working in that company.*

11. *Drugs and alcohol*

Drugs and alcohol can kill your dreams. We have seen this happening to our friends, relatives, neighbours, colleagues, or people we know. Drugs and alcohol killed their dreams. If you are not careful, you might find yourself amongst that list of people whose dreams were killed by drugs and alcohol.

When you have conversations with some of the people who are addicted to drugs or whose lives were destroyed by drugs, some of them will share with you what they desired to achieve or what their dreams were before they got addicted to drugs. Some of them dropped out of school or left their jobs. They abandoned their dreams and allowed drugs to kill those dreams.

The same applies to those who are addicted to alcohol. Some had great dreams, such as playing soccer, being musicians, professors, etc. But because of their inability to control their drinking, none of their dreams came true.

Drugs and alcohol can have negative effects on your life that can prevent you from reaching your full potential and achieving your dreams, which is why it is important to stay away from drugs and alcohol and focus on leading a healthy, productive, and fulfilling life.

Let your dreams matter the most to you, and let them discipline and help you live a life that will not kill those dreams.

Most people started by saying, *"I am having fun."* Unfortunately, that fun became an addiction. Some were busy pleasing their so-called friends because they didn't want to be called *"boring friends."* Sadly, they are not boring but addicted to drugs or alcohol, and they have forgotten about their dreams.

Painfully so, some of those friends they were pleasing are not addicted to drugs or alcohol but are achieving their dreams and succeeding. Or we can say they are *addicted* to success and living and enjoying their lives to the fullest. *How painful is it to destroy your life trying to please others?*

Don't allow drugs and alcohol to kill your dreams. Don't allow having fun or not wanting to be called or seen as boring to destroy your life. *Never destroy your life trying to please others, especially your so-called friends.*

12. A lack of resources

In order for you to achieve your dreams, you need resources such as time, money, skills, and support. Not having access to these resources can be a huge obstruction on your journey to success. It can lead to helplessness and disappointment and even cause you to give up on your dreams altogether.

I have faced that several times, and unfortunately, it delayed my dreams from being achieved on my set time. Luckily, it delayed my dreams but did not kill them as it did most people. I managed to achieve my dreams, such as writing and publishing this book, even though I struggled with funds.

It can be frustrating and demotivating to face a lack of resources, but the good news is that there are ways to work around this challenge. You can approach this by identifying alternative resources to help you achieve your dreams.

For example, if you lack funds to start a business, you can look for grants, loans, or investors who can support your venture. If you lack the skills to pursue your chosen career, you can enrol in training programs, take online courses, or seek mentorship from experienced professionals. You can look for a job and fund your dreams with your salary.

You can also re-evaluate your dreams and adjust them to align with the resources you have. That requires carefully assessing your priorities and a willingness to be flexible and adapt to changing circumstances. It may also mean being patient and taking small steps towards your dreams instead of trying to make big leaps all at once.

Finally, it is important to remember that a lack of resources does not have to be the end of your dreams. With persistence, creativity, and a willingness to explore new options, you can overcome such a challenge and make your dreams a reality. *Don't allow a lack of resources to kill your dreams.*

13. *Self-doubt*

Have you ever felt like you are your own worst enemy while pursuing your dreams or feeling like you are stopping yourself from pursuing and achieving your dreams?

That is how I often felt. I found myself to be the one standing between myself and achieving my dreams. I doubted myself and talked myself out of what I was planning to do or achieve. I was my worst enemy, delaying progress towards achieving my dreams, and I almost gave up on them. Fortunately, I realised that problem and overcame it.

One example is that I delayed writing this book. I doubted myself and made all the excuses I could come up with, and at some point, I felt discouraged to continue with it. Luckily, I remembered why I was writing it, and that helped me overcome the self-doubt that was tormenting and distracting me.

"Self-doubt is a dream killer. And if you don't face and overcome it, it will kill your dreams."

When you constantly doubt yourself and your abilities, it can negatively affect your dreams. Self-doubt can create a mental barrier and prevent you from taking the necessary steps and risks and confidently pursuing your dreams. It can lead to a lack of motivation and ultimately cause you to give up on your dreams.

Therefore, it is essential to recognise and address your self-doubt. That way, you will overcome it and achieve your dreams. It will often be there, but don't let it hold you back from achieving your dreams and living your life to the fullest. *Don't let it kill your dreams and destroy your life.*

14. *Your lifestyle*

Your dreams are important and require you to pursue them with passion and dedication. It is crucial to remember that the lifestyle you choose can either be a motivation or an obstacle to achieving your dreams.

Your daily habits and choices can move you towards achieving your dreams or hold you back. And when you prioritise activities and behaviours that don't align with your dreams, you may struggle to make meaningful progress and think your dreams are out of reach.

If you feel stuck or unable to progress towards achieving your dreams, take a closer look at your lifestyle and consider making required adjustments that align more closely with your plans and dreams.

By prioritising activities and behaviours that support your dreams, you can create a fulfilling life that is both rewarding and empowering. Remember, the power to make your dreams a reality lies within you. Your habits and choices play a significant role in this regard. *Therefore, don't let your lifestyle kill your dreams.*

15. **YOU** can be a dream killer and kill your dreams.

Yes! **YOU.** You can be the one who destroys your dreams, or in other words, *you can be a dream killer.*

That means you may have dreams, desires, and goals you want to achieve. But you engage in self-sabotaging behaviours or negative thinking patterns that prevent you from achieving those dreams, desires, and goals.

Sometimes, you might be afraid of failure or doubt your abilities, and these beliefs can hold you back. Therefore, it is important to recognise when you are limiting yourself in this manner so that you can take steps to overcome such obstacles and pursue your dreams with confidence and determination.

The way you think and talk to yourself is critical because if your thoughts are negative and you speak negatively about yourself or to yourself, you will reap negative results, which might lead to your dreams being killed.

Your lack of discipline, commitment, consistency, and perseverance can kill your dreams. Having dreams but not planning and taking action to achieve them can make you a dream killer and kill your dreams.

Comfort zone, laziness, and procrastination can kill your dreams. The more you keep saying, I will or delaying planning and taking action, the more years pass without your dreams achieved, and you end up giving up on them. In other words, *"You end up killing your dreams."*

Remember that you are in charge of your life and responsible for achieving your dreams and living your life to the fullest. You are the one to protect your dreams against all the mentioned dream killers, and if you don't do that, those dream killers will kill your dreams, and you will be the one to blame because you did not protect your dreams.

"Instead of being a dream killer, protect your dreams against dream killers."

Otherwise, you will have dreams that will never come true because they will be delayed and killed by dream killers. Never allow anything or anyone to stop you from having dreams, achieving them, and living your life to the fullest. Your dreams are unique. Nobody can make them come true except you.

Stay focused and determined. Get out of your comfort zone and laziness and push forward to a better life that achieving your dreams can give you. *Please don't kill your dreams; achieve them.*

How can you protect your dreams against dream killers?

Be aware that dream killers are there and are after your dreams to make sure they never come true. Every chance they get, they will hit you and check if you are indeed committed to your dreams. And if you are not, that will be their chance to kill your dreams.

Never let anyone dim your light or discourage you from following your dreams. There will always be challenges throughout your journey. There will always be naysayers, some of whom may claim to protect you or to have your best interests at heart. Others may be intimidated by your potential success.

But remember this, *"You are the only one who can make your dreams a reality. They are yours, and only you can achieve them."* So, be selective about whose opinions you take to heart.

Keep your head up and be focused on achieving your dreams and living your life to the fullest. *Protecting your dreams is essential. Never overlook it.*

Here are some ways to protect your dreams:
1. Pray and ask God to help you to be aware and overcome dream killers that might want to kill your dreams. Ask Him to protect your dreams and never let anything destroy them.

2. Surround yourself with positive people who support and encourage you. Avoid those who doubt or belittle you and your dreams.

3. Be aware of your negative self-talk and replace it with positive affirmations. Focus on your strengths and progress rather than your weaknesses.

4. Do write down your dreams and make a plan to achieve them. Break them into

smaller, achievable steps, and celebrate your successes as you progress. That will encourage you to keep going.

5. You can stay motivated and inspired by reading books, listening to educational and inspiring recordings, or watching videos that align with your dreams.

6. Finally, never let setbacks or failures discourage you. Use them as learning opportunities, and keep progressing towards achieving your dreams.

Be careful who you share your dreams with and whoever you find yourself sharing your dreams with, pay attention to their response, and observe if it encourages you to achieve your dreams or kill them.

Make sure that you protect your dreams against dream killers, and don't let them kill your dreams. Never let them stop you from achieving your dreams and living your life to the fullest.

Yes! You will face dream killers, but like any other challenge, face and overcome them. *You have what it takes to do that.*

Chapter 4

Overcome the unexpected and discouragement

"Challenges won't give you a notice that they are coming your way. They will just hit you unexpectedly." - **PuleSir**

Yes! You will face the unexpected while pursuing your dreams. You will be disappointed and discouraged. But does that mean you should give up on your dreams? **No!**

Giving up should not be a solution or an option you opt for when you encounter life's challenges or when the unexpected takes place in your life. Use those challenges as an opportunity to learn, grow, improve, and be a better person.

Say to yourself, *"Giving up is not an option for me. I cannot give up."*

The truth is that life has many challenges, and sometimes, those challenges can be discouraging and depressing. They can cause you to ask yourself now and again if your dreams are worth fighting for, and if you are uncertain about why you have those dreams, you will give up when challenges hit you hard.

Setbacks and challenges are an unavoidable aspect of life. At some point, you will face them, whether it is a setback in your career, a personal disappointment, sickness, or financial struggle.

But always remember that every setback is an opportunity for you to learn and grow. And with perseverance and determination, you can overcome anything that comes your way.

Never let challenges and discouragement hold you back. Instead, face them head-on and keep progressing towards achieving your dreams.

It is important how you respond to challenges. If you want to succeed, you must learn to respond by facing and overcoming them and keep pushing forward, no matter how difficult they seem. Never respond by quitting or running away from them. *But respond by facing and overcoming whichever challenge you face.*

The unexpected does take place in life

Throughout the journey of my life, I learned that things don't always go as planned. Sometimes, they take an unplanned or unexpected turn. And when that happens, we may feel bitter, confused, and lose focus. *That is why most people had great dreams but never achieved them.*

They could not overcome the unexpected that took place in their lives. They could not handle failure and the challenges they came across. They gave up just because things did not go their way. When the unexpected took place in their lives, they failed to pick up the pieces and continue with their journey.

The unexpected almost destroyed my dreams

After completing my matric in 2004, I dreamed of becoming an author. I wanted to write two Setswana books *(Poetry and a Novel)*. With them, I wanted to inspire people and address our day-to-day challenges.

In 2007, I started writing a poetry book, **"Go rileng Bagaetsho?"** Simply asking, *"What happened?"* Looking into all that we go through in our day-to-day lives, like *"Crime, abuse, rape, poverty, unemployment, etc."* By then, I was using a pencil and writing in a flash book, and I completed 80 poems by 2012.

While I was busy writing that poetry book, I also started writing the novel, **"Pelong ke botlhoko."** Simply saying, *"I am heartbroken."* Also, because of the challenges we go through in our day-to-day lives. I was writing each book on its flash book.

After writing both books, I got access to a computer, where I typed and edited them. I then saved them on that computer and waited for the right time to publish them.

Unfortunately, as the unexpected often takes place in our lives uninvited, somewhere during the beginning of 2014, the year I planned to publish those two books, the computer that I saved them on crashed, and everything on it, including my books, was lost.

I thought I was daydreaming, but unfortunately, I was not. I lost all the work that I had been writing. *What a tragedy!*

"Challenges will hit you unexpectedly and will tear you apart. But regardless of all that, pick up the pieces and move on with your life."

It felt as if my life had crashed. I was hurt, disappointed, and not sure what to do or think. I kept asking, *"How did all that happen, and why did it happen that way?"* Unfortunately, no one answered me, and I didn't even know who to talk to at that time.

I had to accept that the unexpected came uninvited into my life and took my books. It was not easy, and I felt like a part of me had just died.

Hurting, discouraged, and feeling hopeless

I had no energy to continue writing. Even though the work I wrote in the flash books was still available, it was not the same because, during the typing process, I gave it my all. I edited and added more content to complete those books, and losing all that was a huge and painful setback.

Being hurt like that made me feel like I could give up on those books and let them go, but that dream kept on saying, *"I am still here. You must write those books again and many more that you are destined to write."*

I prayed and asked God to give me the strength to write those books again. I then took the flash books and read what I wrote several times, hoping to find inspiration.

But it was hard, and that feeling of giving up and forgetting about writing those books returned once more, saying, *"What's the point? Let it go."* But I refused to give up, no matter how painful it was.

Since I was hurt and confused, I decided to put that dream on hold to allow myself to heal from that tragedy and regain my strength to write those books. *And indeed, I did regain that strength.*

Always remember the following,

- Don't give up on your dreams when you face challenges.
- Things will happen in your life unexpectedly and uninvited. But don't let them destroy you.
- You will face challenges, and you will find yourself in situations where you would not even know how you got there, but don't ever give up on your dreams, and don't ever give up on yourself and in life.
- Don't ever be stuck in pain when happiness is out there, waiting for you to pursue and enjoy.

You have to refuse to give up, no matter what

I almost got stuck in the pain of losing my books, but I refused. I nearly gave up on my dream of becoming an author, but I refused regardless of what happened to me. I had to pick up the pieces and move on with my life. It was not easy, but I had to. Otherwise, I was going to be stuck with what happened to me instead of focusing on what I could do since the unexpected took place uninvited in my life.

After that painful incident of losing my books, I immediately bought myself a laptop. I started using *Dropbox* to save my files. So that even if the laptop crashed, I could still access those files.

Besides writing those two books, I also wrote inspirational posts for my Facebook account, the Agape Youth Movement Facebook page, and other social media platforms. Even after losing my books, I continued writing those posts. And that led me to write and publish my first book, **"Beyond Inspiration,"** which I co-authored with Thabang Phala, known as **"Abuti Rams,"** in 2015.

After writing and publishing Beyond Inspiration, I felt good and proud of myself. And that inspired me to write books inside of me, including those two Setswana books I lost when the computer crashed. You will read them one day, as I chose to publish this one before them.

But why am I sharing this with you?

I am doing that because I want you to know that we all go through challenges in life. I want you to know that things don't always go as we plan or as we want them to. Sometimes they do, but other times they take the unexpected way.

Unfortunately, when that happens, we get hurt, disappointed, and sometimes feel like giving up on pursuing our dreams or in life.

I want you to know that you will get tired, disappointed, and discouraged while pursuing your dreams. You will discourage yourself, people will discourage you, situations will discourage you, and the unexpected will also discourage you. *But regardless of all that, never give up on your dreams.*

Never let the unexpected and discouragements destroy you, and never give up when they take place in your life. You must always remember your dreams and where you are going. And let that inspire and motivate you not to give up but to keep going forward until you achieve your dreams.

I might not know which plans failed in your life, but don't give up on them. I might not know the unexpected that took place in your life and left you bleeding and disappointed. I might not know the discouragement you faced or are still facing, but *never give up on your dreams.*

Cry if you must, or be sad. It is okay. But don't stay in that situation. Continue to pray and ask God to strengthen you and help you to dream again, and you will overcome all that you are going through. *Don't stop believing in your dreams and in yourself to achieve those dreams.*

Always remember, *"The unexpected situations or events won't ask you if they should take place in your life or not. They will just happen, but don't let them take you down. Face and overcome them. Be ready to pick up the pieces and move on with your life every time you fall or every time the unexpected takes place in your life."*

Achieve your dreams in the midst of challenges

When faced with the unexpected or discouragement, it is easy to lose motivation and feel like giving up. But don't let the unpredictable circumstances and discouragement get the best of you. Instead, try these simple tips to help you get back on track and keep moving forward.

Firstly, take a moment to reflect on what went wrong and why it happened. This will help you identify areas for improvement and avoid making the same mistakes in the future.

Next, break down your dreams into smaller and achievable tasks. This will help you gain momentum and build confidence as you progress towards achieving your dreams.

Additionally, feel free to seek support from friends, family, or a professional. Sometimes, talking about your challenges with someone else can provide a fresh perspective and renewed motivation.

Finally, remember to be kind to yourself and celebrate your successes, no matter how small they may seem. Challenges and discouragement are a natural part of any journey. But with perseverance and a positive mindset, you can overcome any obstacle and achieve your dreams.

Never allow the unexpected and discouragement to stop you from achieving your dreams. You must confidently face and overcome them and make sure your dreams come true.

Chapter 5

Don't lose hope, and don't give up

"We fail in life, but we don't give up because our goals are greater than our failures." - **PuleSir**

When you lose hope, your life worsens, and stress hits you from all corners. And when you give up, your life gets filled with regrets, and depression takes over and destroys you.

"It might be challenging or rough for you, but don't lose hope, and don't give up."

The truth is that as much as we have dreams, ideas, and the ability to visualise our success and the future we desire, none of us really know or are sure that it will happen that way. *We want it to, we wish and plan it to, but we are not sure it will happen that way.*

We don't want to meet challenges and don't plan to have setbacks while pursuing our dreams. All we want is to achieve our dreams, be successful, enjoy and live our lives to the fullest. *We are happy and excited about the final product that we visualised.*

Because of that, it becomes painful and discouraging for us when the unexpected takes place in our lives. We somehow find it hard to handle and live beyond that because we never considered it. We never considered the unexpected setbacks and challenges we might face while pursuing our dreams.

Unfortunately, that is where most people fail in life. They fail to handle the unexpected and to live beyond what they face along the journey. Sadly, their dreams and visions die before they can be accomplished. *They lose hope and give up on their dreams and on themselves.*

Let us not join them or be like them, but let us know and be aware that failure and challenges exist in life. We will face them. We will be tested many times in our endeavour to achieve our dreams and live our lives to the fullest. But we have to live beyond all that.

We have to fight and conquer anything that will stand in the way of our success. Otherwise, we will only have dreams and visualise our future but never accomplish anything.

"Never give up or quit no matter how hard and challenging the journey is." **- PuleSir**

The Dream vs. Reality

"What you see or dream of versus what could happen or what you can face while pursuing your dreams."

Remember that challenges won't care or be intimidated by your dream no matter how great it is. You will face them, and if you are not strong enough or committed to achieving your dream, you will give up and never achieve that dream.

The Dream

Let us say, for example, that your dream from a young age may be to perform exceptionally well in your studies up to matric, receive a bursary to further your studies after matric, enrol in your preferred university, pursue your favourite course, and complete your studies.

After all that, your dream continues to be finding employment in your field of study and, above all, being the happiest and most successful person in the world. Furthermore, you can meet the people you have always wanted to meet, travel worldwide, live in your dream home, drive your favourite car, and enjoy life to the fullest, just the way you desire.

That might be something you desire or dream of, and it is indeed a great dream and a promising future you can have.

"You should write your dream down, internalise it, and keep playing it when you face life's challenges or when the unexpected takes place in your life."

That way, it can keep you encouraged and motivated moving forward because life is not as obvious and straightforward as you dream of it or want it to be.

The truth is that your dream can be great, but it can now and then be challenged and leave you hopeless and wondering what really happened and where it all went wrong.

Your future might look promising, but challenges can hit you hard and leave you wondering if your dreams will come true and if you will have the future you anticipate having.

The Reality

The unexpected can happen in your life and change everything, causing confusion and delays and leaving you wondering what really happened.

That time is when your dream gets crushed. When the dream you had about performing exceptionally well in your studies, receiving a bursary, studying your favourite course, and being employed in your field of study gets crushed.

When the exemption you dreamed of passing with becomes symbol S. Your subjects' marks drop in a way that makes it impossible for you to get a bursary, to be accepted at the university, and study your anticipated course, meaning you won't be able to study, and qualify for it and be employed for that job you desired.

All now seems impossible to achieve. Your vision starts to fade away, and your dreams become nightmares to you, giving you sleepless nights.

You start losing hope and have no strength to give it another try because everything you try seems to fall apart. But you keep telling yourself that you can. You will achieve your dreams regardless of all that happened. You promise yourself that you will give it another try.

You register for a particular course at the college, but for some reason known to yourself, you don't complete it. You think of putting your studies on hold and start looking for a job to make money. You sent as many CVs and emails as possible to different companies, but sadly, nobody responded.

By all means, you try to hold yourself together and stay positive, believing that things will work out for you, but day by day, things are getting worse.

You have patiently waited for the day of your breakthrough, but that day seems to be scared of you, as to this point, it has not arrived. Your positive attitude slowly turns into a negative one. You begin to think that maybe those dreams were never meant for you, or maybe you did not see your vision clearly.

You start believing all the negatives people told you and conclude that the vision you once sat down and visualised and the dreams you had were not for you. Cursing the moment you believed and were excited about all that.

That is where most people previously killed their ideas, dreams, and visions. And they never lived to taste the joy and fulfilment of success.

Unfortunately, that is where, even today, most people continue to lose it all, throwing in the towel and giving up on chasing their beautiful dreams. They fail to see the light at the end of the tunnel and to understand that challenges are part of life. *They are supposed to build them and direct them to where they are going, not to destroy them or to end their journey.*

When they see years passing while still struggling, they lose hope and easily give up on the wonderful life they desired. They stop dreaming, being active and excited about life and their plans, and, just like that, they give up and settle for a mediocre life.

I want to emphasise this: *"You will face challenges while pursuing your dreams,"* but don't allow them to destroy or stop you from achieving those dreams.

Never allow them to knock you down, no matter how hard they hit you. Take them as a test or a refinement, refining you to be the best you are supposed to be.

Also, remember this, *"You will fail at some point in your life,"* but that does not mean you are a failure and should give up. It simply means, *"Take the lesson, improve, and move on to the next chapter of your life."*

Close the previous chapter and move on to a new one with the attitude that says, *"Yes, I failed, but I learned my lesson and will continue with my journey towards achieving my dreams."*

You will face challenges while pursuing your dreams

The truth is that challenges will come your way. And there are times when you will have to travel on rough roads with potholes, humps, and accidents while pursuing your dreams.

You will come across heavy storms pushing you away from your dreams and challenges, challenging your abilities and strength. You will have negative people telling you now and again that you can't and won't achieve your dreams or make it in life.

"You will fail, fall, be discouraged, and be disappointed. And you will come across closed and locked doors with no one welcoming you in."

That is the reality and the truth we miss when visualising our lives or setting goals. Unfortunately, when we come across such situations, they hit us so hard that some of us don't stand up again after such stumbling blocks of life.

They break us into pieces that many have failed to pick themselves up from and continue with their journey to their destinations. That is why we often hear people saying, *"If only. I should have, I wish I could, I regret....."*

They have many regrets, and it's painful for them as they are not living the lives they wanted. They are living the opposite of the lives they wanted to live because of the challenges they faced, which they failed to overcome.

Persevere and never give up

If you could read stories of the most successful people you may be looking up to or following, you would realise that as much as they are successful, their journey was not as smooth as we think, yet they made it and achieved their dreams.

Some, when you read their stories, you would realise that, if you were in their shoes, you could have given up, but they did not because they made a commitment that they would achieve their dreams, and they certainly did.

"How hard can it be for you to do the same? To persevere and never give up."

You can, and you will achieve your dreams and make your vision a reality, but it is not as simple as you think when visualising your life from **Point A** to **Point B.** As such, be prepared for your journey to your destination. *Be willing to* *persevere and never give up when it gets challenging.*

Do your thorough research and be aware of the delays and obstructions you might encounter along the way. So that when you meet them, they won't destroy your dreams. You will be able to face and overcome them and continue with your journey until you achieve your dream.

You are not a failure

Never lose hope or give up on your dreams and the life you want to live because there is always a way forward after unexpected situations. Never give up on your dreams, no matter the challenges you face or how long it takes to achieve those dreams.

Don't lose hope, and don't give up. Pray and ask God to help you overcome anything that wants to delay you and cause you to give up on your dreams. He placed those dreams in your heart for a reason, and He can help you to achieve them.

Don't let challenges stop you from achieving your dreams. But face and overcome them. Don't be defeated by them, but defeat them and achieve your dreams. *You can do that.*

Set goals or dreams with an open mind. Do your thorough research, looking into all the possibilities that can make your goals or dreams fail and those that will make them come true. That way, you can know what to expect along the way and have other options to consider if you face challenges.

"Don't lose hope, and don't give up on your dreams when you face challenges while pursuing them."

Chapter 6

It is not over with you. Don't give up

"You are an overcomer and a conqueror, not a failure overpowered by life's challenges."
- **PuleSir**

I thought it was over with me when I lost the manuscripts of my Setswana books, but it was not. I thought my dream of becoming an author was over, but it was not. I did not give up when I faced challenges and when the situation was painful. But I persevered. And I achieved my dream and became the author I dreamed of becoming.

I want to remind you that *it is not over with you. Don't give up.* You can still turn things around and achieve your dreams. You can still have the desires of your heart and be the best that God created you to be. But that can only happen when you don't give up or when you rise every time you fall.

When things seem complicated, and you feel like you have hit a dead end, it is important to remember that *it is not over*. Giving up might seem like the easiest or best option, but it is not. It is not the only choice you have.

There is always another way forward, another path you can take, or another opportunity to explore. So, even when you feel like you cannot go on, don't give up, but keep pushing forward.

Keep looking for solutions, and believe in yourself. As long as you keep doing all that, you will overcome whatever you face and achieve your dreams.

"You can achieve your dreams, even if the path to success may not always be clear."

Always remember that success takes time and effort, and setbacks are unavoidable. However, that should never discourage you from pursuing and achieving your dreams. Instead, use those setbacks as opportunities to learn and grow. Let them help you find your true potential and be the best you are born to be.

Remember that you have the ability and strength to overcome any challenge. *You are a conqueror and unstoppable.*

Hold on to your dreams

You might have experienced pain and dissatisfaction, or the unexpected might have occurred in your life, leaving you feeling bitter, sad, stressed, worthless, and hopeless.

You might be at a point in your life where things are complicated and confusing, and you are saying to yourself, *"I can't continue with this anymore. I am giving up."*

I am here today through this book to say, *"It is not over with you. Don't give up on your dreams and the life you desire. You can still make it happen. You can still achieve your dreams no matter what you are going through."*

Those dreams are yours to achieve. They are the reason why you are still alive. They are your purpose in this world to fulfil and your life to live and to enjoy. *Hold on to them.*

If you give up on them, nobody will achieve them. And not only will you fail and disappoint yourself. But you will also fail and disappoint God, who trusted you to achieve those dreams. You will fail the people He sent you to—for you to make a difference in their lives through achieving your dreams.

Your dreams are important, and you need to achieve them. Please, don't give up, don't quit, and don't let go of them. But hold on tight to them because you can achieve them no matter what. *You have what it takes to make them come true.*

It might seem impossible to you now, but it is possible. You are an inspiration and a mentor that many look up to. Don't fail them, but show them that it is possible to have dreams, to achieve them, and to live your life to the fullest regardless of all the setbacks you face.

> *"What good will it do for you if you give up on your dreams and in life?"*

Find the strength to get up again

It might be painful for you, but don't give up. The journey might have setbacks and challenges, but don't give up. Things might not make sense, or your dreams might take longer to come true, but don't give up. *Find the strength to keep moving forward and to get up every time you fall.*

Believe me, I know it is painful. I have experienced that along the journey of my life. I know how it feels to have great dreams but struggle to achieve them. *Dreaming but not achieving your dreams.*

I know the struggle and the pain of watching your peers succeed while you struggle to progress in your own life. Watching your former classmates, whom you outperformed, succeed in achieving their dreams while your own life grows more complicated every day.

What about that one classmate who repeated almost every class, but today, they are successful, and you, on the other hand, are still dreaming of being successful? *That is heart-breaking to experience.*

I know the pain of seeing people younger than you prosper in life while you are not, the pain of watching them use their gifts, skills, ideas, and creative minds to overcome poverty and unemployment and succeed—while you are struggling and not breaking through to a better life.

I know the pain of seeing them employed in big companies, owning businesses, driving the latest model cars, using the latest phones, marrying or being married, living glamorous lives, and living their lives in a way you dreamed of living yours.

Unfortunately, for you, it is the opposite. You are still dreaming and wishing for your dreams to come true. You constantly ask yourself, *"Why can't I be like them and live my life to the fullest?"*

Looking at where you are, you realise you are still far from living that life. You still wake up every day to look for employment or do that job you hate, just to survive.

There is no motivation to keep you going, no joy, and you see nothing to make you happy and appreciate being alive. Stress, loneliness, and depression are now your best friends, draining your energy every day.

Whenever you see someone doing what you dream of doing, you ask yourself, *"Why can't I achieve my dreams and enjoy life like this person? Maybe this was not for me. Maybe I am cursed, bewitched, or maybe I chose the wrong career, and I should try something else."* You ask yourself endless and painful questions with no answers.

Your life will turn around positively

Allow me to give you good news today, *"You did not choose the wrong career. You are not cursed or bewitched. You are just passing through a detour to your destination. Things will work together for good in your life. Hold on a little longer."*

Instead of focusing on the negatives in your life, concentrate on the lessons they present. And instead of giving up, keep pushing forward until you make it in life. If others can do it, surely you can, too.

In you, there is a warrior, and warriors never give up until they achieve their dreams or the goals they set to achieve. They never doubt themselves because they know that all things are possible. And they have what it takes to make their dreams come true despite facing different challenges.

They know that nothing happens in their lives unless that thing has a purpose. Don't let that warrior in you live and die poor because of life's challenges. You are greater than that.

"Whatever you face in life, take it as a stepping stone getting you closer to your destination, not as a stumbling block that blocks your way, making it hard for you to pass through to your success."

- PuleSir

The truth is that we want to progress in life and live the lives we desire. We want to achieve our goals and make our dreams come true. We want to fulfil our purposes and deliver what God sent us to deliver to this world. We want to be educated, employed, or have our businesses.

We want to be successful, significant, and wealthy. We want to be happy and enjoy our lives to the fullest. We wish and want only the best in our lives. But sometimes, things don't go our way, and we find ourselves far from achieving all that we want to achieve. We find ourselves faced with a pile of challenges instead of succeeding.

"If that is the case in your life, know that it is not over with you. It is part of the plan. And if your plans did not go as you envisioned or even if you fell or failed, it is not over with you. It is not over with your life, and it is not over with your plans and your dreams. Rise and continue with your journey."

I see challenges as a test to see how serious and committed we are and how far we are willing to go to achieve our dreams or all that we plan and desire to achieve. They often bring out the best in us. They force us to think, analyse, and learn. We emerge from them better than before and ready to face anything.

It is not over with you. Don't give up, don't lose hope, and don't stop dreaming. But keep on praying and moving forward. Keep on picking yourself up every time you stumble. Keep doing your best, and you will make your plans come true and be successful.

You will live the life you desire, only if you decide today that you won't give up no matter what you come across along your journey to your desired destination.

Let go and be free to move on

Let go of what is holding you back in life and the things you wish you could have again because they are gone for good. Let go of the company that fired or retrenched you. Let go of the relationship that didn't work and everything holding you back.

Let go of the past that you are holding on to and open your hands and heart to receive what God wants to give you now. Open your ears to hear what He is saying and where He is directing you.

God has your back

You might have been praying for a long time but haven't received what you prayed for. Don't give up because God is still busy developing and preparing you for what you asked for. *He is taking His time to answer you for a reason.*

Empty your hands. So you can receive what God has in store for you. Be it your blessings or answers to what you have been praying for.

God knew that you would go through all that you are going through right now. And you would want to give up on yourself, your dreams, and your life. And that is why He said in **Deuteronomy 31:6,** *"Be strong and courageous; don't be terrified or afraid of them. For it is the Lord your God who goes with you; he will not leave you nor forsake you."*

If He promised you that, He will surely do it. Because He is faithful to His word and loves and cares about you. He will heal you, help you, take care of you, give you the desires of your heart, and do exceedingly abundantly above all that you can ask or think of, according to the power that works within you.

None of what you are going through surprises Him, and it is not greater than Him. So trust Him, and don't let it destroy you.

No matter what you will face while pursuing your dreams, remember that it will not be the end of your journey. It will not be over with you, and it will not be over with your dreams. Therefore, *never give up.*

It is not over with you. Don't give up

Everything happens for a reason

On December 1, 2021, I announced on my Facebook account that my Second book, *"Never Give Up on your Dreams,"* would be coming soon.

This is what I said on that Facebook Post,

"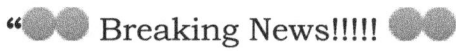 Breaking News!!!!!

After taking some time off after publishing my first book, "Beyond Inspiration,"
I am happy to announce that I am done with my second book, *"Never Give Up on your Dreams."*

I wrote it to inspire and help you to never give up on your dreams no matter the challenges, disappointments, and pain that you will come across or go through along the way. It's time for you to live your life to the fullest, no matter what.

Pre-Order @ R200.00 and be the first to get your copy. The book is available on Amazon.

Share! Share! Share! And alert 🔴 your friends. Link to Amazon: https://amzn.to/3p12qQA"

I was excited. After all, I had been working on that book for some time. I edited it and created its cover. I even converted it to an eBook and published it on Amazon.

My social media friends congratulated me, and others shared the post with their friends, helping me spread the message about my upcoming book.

> *"I was happy and proud of myself. It was a dream come true for me."*

I asked my friends to pre-order the book so that I would know who to send a copy to when it was published. I also needed that money for pre-orders to publish the book, as I did not have the funds.

The plan was to promote the book during December so that it would be published and ready by January 2022. It was going to be my birthday present on January 11.

Unfortunately, things did not go as I planned. Nobody pre-ordered the book. Some promised to pre-order or to get the eBook, but none kept their promise.

No matter what, never give up

I was disappointed. Since I received so many congratulations, I thought people would pre-order the book or purchase the eBook on Amazon, but none of that happened.

I tried different strategies to promote the book and the eBook, but none worked. Only one person bought the eBook—*my former colleague at Madibeng FM*—directly from me, not from Amazon.

I was discouraged and kept asking myself, *"What is the plan now?"* I could not answer that question or come up with a plan except to say, *"Things will work out just fine."*

I left things like that, not knowing what to do next. But I believed that they would work out just fine.

One thing I promised myself was that I would never give up on that dream. After all, the book was titled *"Never Give Up on your Dreams."* So, there was no way I was going to give up on that book unless what was written in it was not working.

I mean, how do you give up while telling others not to give up?

Some asked about the book, and I told them I paused with it as I wanted to edit some parts of it. I could not tell them the truth as I felt embarrassed about all that happened.

Why do I say, "Everything happens for a reason?"

While figuring out what to do, I stumbled upon a book titled *"The Scribe Method."* The book teaches how to write a book, from having an idea to writing an actual book. While reading that book, I realised I made too many mistakes while writing mine. These things reminded me that *"Everything happens for a reason, even if you don't understand that reason at that time."*

For example, I did not know who my actual reader was. I did not structure the book accordingly, and there were too many things I did not do right. I learned a lot from that book, which I did not know before writing mine.

This is what I realised and why I say everything happens for a reason,
1. If people pre-ordered the book, I would not give it to them on time as I did not have the funds to publish it. This was going to destroy

my image and the trust those pre-ordered had in me.

2. If I had succeeded in publishing the book by then, it would have had many mistakes and not fulfilled its purpose accordingly. There is a huge difference and improvement between the one you are reading and the one I wrote before.

As I am writing this part, it is May 11, 2024, almost three years after I announced that my book was coming. But here I am, rewriting and reediting it. It has not been published.

You can imagine the embarrassment, disappointment, and pain I encountered. I mean, how do you say something is coming soon, and three years later, you are still working on that thing?

With this story, I want to say to you, *"You will plan, and sometimes things will go as you planned, but at other times, they will take a way you never expected. When that happens, never give up.*

"You will be discouraged and disappointed because of how things happened, but know that everything happens for a reason, even if, at that time, you don't understand that reason."

If my book had been published then, many things you have read or will read would not have been there. If I had given up when I could not raise the funds to publish this book, you would not be reading it.

I never gave up on my dream, no matter what obstacles I faced while pursuing it. *And I want to encourage you to do the same.*

This book proves that you can have a dream and face challenges while pursuing it. You can face those challenges and become a conqueror with your dream achieved.

Maybe you have already given up on your dream. But I challenge you to dig deep inside yourself and find the strength to get up again and pursue your dream until you achieve it. *You have that dream for a reason.*

I want you to know that it is not over with you. Get up, get out there, and make things happen. Pursue your dreams and achieve them. *You can do that.*

Delays are not denial

"Delays to achieve your dreams are not a denial of your dreams. Overcome those delays and achieve your dreams." **- PuleSir**

Experiencing delays as you work towards achieving your dreams should not be seen as a sign that your dreams won't come true. Instead, view these delays as temporary obstacles you can overcome and continue with your journey to achieving your dreams.

It is important to remember that encountering delays in achieving our dreams is not the same as being denied the opportunity to pursue them. Although delays can be frustrating and discouraging, they are a natural part of the journey towards achieving our dreams.

One of the essential characteristics of successful people is their ability to recognise these delays and not let them derail their progress. They keep pushing forward, even when things get tough.

They are not afraid to think creatively and look for alternative solutions when the path to their dreams is blocked. They may also seek help and guidance from others who have overcome similar challenges.

When we face delays, it is easy to feel like we are not making progress or we are failing. But it is important to remember that delays are not permanent roadblocks.

With a positive attitude and perseverance, we can find ways to overcome delays and continue our journey towards achieving our dreams.

Ultimately, the satisfaction of achieving our dreams is worth the effort and strength required to get there. So, keep pushing forward, stay focused, and don't let delays discourage you. Remember that success is not always a straight line but a winding path with obstacles to overcome.

The pain of not achieving your dreams

Achieving your dreams will bring you satisfaction and happiness. It will give you the things you want to have and the life you desire to live. You will be proud of yourself and be an inspiration to many or to those who look up to you.

But if you fail to achieve your dreams, regrets, pain, feelings of disappointment, and frustration will crush you hard.

The pain of not achieving your dreams can be overwhelming and affect every aspect of your life, from personal relationships to professional endeavours. It is a challenging situation to be in.

You live in pain and with regrets. You hate those who achieved their dreams. You are afraid or ashamed to meet people who know your dreams. You are easily irritated and get angry when others ask about your dreams. *That is the pain of not achieving your dreams.*

Failure is painful

When you talk with people, you can feel the pain of not achieving their dreams. When you ask them what happened, you realise that for most of them, the problem is that they failed to protect their dreams against dream killers, and unfortunately, dream killers killed their dreams.

Don't add to that list, but make sure you achieve your dreams so you won't experience *the pain of not achieving your dreams*. Maybe you are about to give up or have already given up, but I want you to rise and achieve your dreams.

"You might be down, but don't stay down. Take yourself up to greatness, not down to mediocrity."
- PuleSir

Chapter 7

The ingredients to achieve your dreams

"Your dreams are waiting for you to take action to achieve them so that they can give you the life you desire to live." - **PuleSir**

Dreams do come true, but they require you *(the dreamer)* to play your part. They won't just happen on their own, but you must take action for them to come true. You need to add all the necessary ingredients to achieve your dreams because if you don't do that, they will remain dreams that never came true.

If you don't play your role in achieving your dreams, you will forever be surprised when you see others achieving theirs and succeeding in life and wonder what they could be doing that you are not.

Here are some of the key ingredients you need to make your dreams come true.

1. *Write your dreams down.*

Habakkuk 2:2-3 says, *"Then the Lord answered me and said, "Write the vision and make it plain on tablets, that he may run who reads it. For the vision is yet for an appointed time, but at the end it will speak and it will not lie. Though it tarries, wait for it, because it will surely come, it will not tarry."*

The book of Habakkuk reminds us to write down our dreams and visions so that we can revisit them and remember where we are going.

Most people use vision boards to help them clarify what they want to achieve and stay focused. They write their dreams down, find pictures that match their dreams, and use those pictures to create a vision board.

Every day, when they wake up, they check their vision boards to draw inspiration for the new day. Even in the evening, some visit their vision boards to remind themselves of their goals and dreams.

These are simple and achievable things you should do if you are committed to making your dreams come true and turning your vision into a reality.

Write your dreams down, and create a vision board to draw inspiration from whenever you get tired or feel discouraged. Seeing your dreams every day will give you the push you need to achieve them. And every time you tick the dreams you have achieved, you will be inspired and encouraged that you can achieve the remaining ones or the ones you will have as time goes on.

2. *ACT* because *A*ction *C*hanges *T*hings

Your dreams are important and worth pursuing. However, having dreams is not enough. You have to achieve them. Wishing for them to come true will not give you results. You have to plan and take action to make them come true.

"Plan and take action. It works." **- PuleSir**

Set goals to ensure a clear roadmap towards achieving your dreams, as dreams without goals are unlikely to be achieved. Goals provide clear directions to move from your current position to your desired destination, *which is the completion of your dreams.*

Break your dreams into achievable goals. Develop a timeline to reach your goals and make your dreams a reality. Track your progress as you take action every day. Doing that will help you build momentum and a sense of accomplishment.

By having a well-defined plan and taking consistent action, you can make your dreams a reality and enjoy the satisfaction that comes with it.

The truth is that nothing comes easily in life. But everything is possible and achievable, and so are your dreams. They can come true, but you need to believe in yourself and believe that you can and will achieve them.

Plan and take action to achieve your dreams. Work hard and take calculated risks where needed to succeed in this world.

I planned and took action to achieve my dream

Years back, I fell in love with radio and dreamed of becoming a radio presenter. I visualised myself achieving that dream and making a difference in other people's lives through radio. I captured that vision to remember where I was going and for it to inspire me when I got tired.

I understood that having a dream is not enough; I had to plan and take action to achieve it. I also remembered that I had to act because action changes things. It can take me from where I was to where I desired to be—*on the radio, presenting a show.* And I did exactly that.

I planned and took action to become a radio presenter, and guess what? I achieved that dream.

Go an extra mile to achieve your dreams

Since I knew nothing about radio presenting, I had to research it and learn everything I could about it. After all the research, I had to take action to implement the advice that I had gathered.

My first step was to put together a script that I intended to use when I went for auditions. I created that script and started rehearsing and internalising it, preparing myself for an opportunity or the auditions.

Unfortunately, months passed without hearing about any auditions. So, **Plan B** was to record that script as a demo and send it to different radio stations. I did that. I booked a recording studio and went there to record my demo.

The guy who helped me with the recording was impressed with the script's content and how I delivered it. His remarks gave me hope and encouragement that the people I will be sending the demo to will also be impressed and give me a chance to be a radio presenter at their radio station.

After recording the demo, I searched for radio stations to which I could send it, and I did that. I sent different emails. *To my surprise, no one responded.* I was shocked, as that was not what I expected.

Some of my friends came through and suggested people to whom we could send that demo, and we did that, but still, *no one responded.* Wow! What a shock. *That was different from what I envisioned.* And when it happened, it hit me hard and caused me to start doubting myself and my ability to be a radio presenter.

I wondered why no one responded, and the only thing that came to mind was the discouraging comment, *"Maybe you don't have what it takes to be a radio presenter."*

But I did not lose hope or give up. I kept rehearsing the script and believing that something positive would come, and indeed, an opportunity came. There were auditions at Kopanong FM in Lehurutshe (North West Province), and I went to audition. Unfortunately, I was not successful in being selected as their presenter.

Even today, I don't know what happened to my voice that day. Something stuck in my throat and prevented me from presenting my script as I prepared or desired. I did not sound convincing to be a radio presenter, and unfortunately, I did not make it.

But since I understood the importance of having that dream and the importance of achieving it. I did not lose hope or give up. I kept on looking for another opportunity.

I emailed another radio station (Aganang FM) in Potchefstroom (North West Province) as I came across a post saying they were looking for presenters. Fortunately, I got called to come and audition. I did my audition and answered the questions, but unfortunately, I was not selected as I never received a call.

Sometimes, I wonder if it was not because of the salary I asked for, as I asked double what they were paying their presenters. But I did not know.

I only asked based on what I was earning from the company I was working for.

Anyhow, I kept the faith. I did not lose hope or give up on my dream of being a radio presenter. I kept on sending emails and searching for auditions. I liked the Facebook pages of different radio stations to see when they have auditions, as most radio stations post that on their Facebook pages.

After some time, I saw a post that Madibeng FM in Brits (North West Province) was looking for presenters and would host auditions. I rehearsed my script and attended the auditions—and did my best.

The programme manager who conducted the auditions was impressed with how I auditioned. He said I had a voice for radio and would call me if I was selected. *That gave me hope.*

The auditions were on a Saturday. On Sunday, the programme manager called me. Unfortunately, I missed his call because I was in a meeting, and my phone was silent. Later, I tried calling him but could not get hold of him. From that moment, I knew deep down that I had missed a lifetime opportunity—my chance to get into radio.

Days went by, and as I listened to that radio station, I could hear new voices. I knew I was supposed to be one of those new voices, but unfortunately, I missed the most important call that would have taken me there.

As I was about to forget about that radio station and accept that I missed my opportunity, the programme manager I missed a call from called me and told me that one of the guys they selected was giving them problems, and I must come in for training so that I could do the show that guy was doing. Indeed, I went, did my best, and everything went well. That was the start of my radio presenting journey. *It was in August 2017.*

And guess what? I emailed that radio station several times before the auditions, submitting my demo. And they never responded to those emails, and there I was, working for that same radio station. But I got in through going for the auditions.

With all this, I want to say to you, *"Dreams do come true."* **Yes!** Sometimes, the journey can take longer than expected. Sometimes, we get rejected where we never thought we would. We knock, and no one opens the door for us. But in the end, we can achieve our dreams if we don't lose hope and give up on them when we face challenges. *We must be persistent.*

Had I given up when no one answered my emails or when I did not succeed with my previous auditions, I would not have achieved my dream of being a radio presenter. However, my commitment and persistence to my dream helped me to enter and succeed in the radio industry.

You, too, can achieve your dreams no matter how many times you will fail or get rejected. Don't give up, but be persistent until you achieve your dreams.

3. *Stay focused and positive*

Avoid setting too many goals, as it may be challenging to keep up with them. This could also lead to distraction and demotivation, which can cause you to give up on your dreams.

Set achievable goals. Remain focused and positive no matter what. There will always be distractions, but don't let them shift your focus from your dreams.

4. Commitment, consistency, and discipline

Remember that achieving your dreams requires commitment, consistency, and discipline. With these three, you can have dreams and achieve them. But without these three, you can have dreams, be excited about them, and plan to achieve them but never achieve them.

These are the things that caused delays in my life. I did not have them, and because of that, I set goals that I did not achieve. I postponed tasks when I was supposed to complete them. I started projects that I did not finish. Or that took longer to complete. *All these happened because I lacked commitment, consistency, and discipline.*

You must be committed to your dreams and consistently take steps to achieve them. You must be disciplined to do what you have to do for your dreams to come true.

You will not go anywhere in life without commitment, consistency, and discipline, and you will surely achieve nothing. The problem with lacking these three ingredients is that you start projects but don't complete them and set goals but never achieve them.

Motivation gets you started, but commitment, consistency, and discipline keep you going. Make sure you include this as you plan to have dreams and achieve them.

5. *Hard work and sacrifice*

Hard work is required if you want your dreams to come true. Sacrifice is also a necessity. Sometimes, you must sacrifice going out with friends and work on your dreams. Other times, you have to sacrifice your sleep and work on accomplishing your dreams.

Through hard work, persistence, and a willingness to learn from your failures, you can take significant steps towards achieving the life you have always envisioned.

> *"Remember that you can transform your dreams into reality with the right ingredients."*

Sacrifice where needed for your dreams to come true, and work hard. Because it takes sweat, determination, and hard work for your dreams to come true. Always remember that *"Things don't just happen. You make them happen."*

6. *Follow your dreams*

Make sure you follow your dreams, not other people's dreams. Often, people fail because they follow other people's dreams. For example, someone saw their colleague succeeding with a particular course, and they registered for it as well and failed because they were pursuing someone else's dreams.

Don't do that if you want to succeed in life. Follow your dreams and stop confusing yourself with other people's dreams. What did God place in your heart? What is it that you want to achieve? That is your dream. Follow it, and you will realise that, indeed, *"Dreams do come true."*

7. *Protect your dreams*

Your dreams are valuable, and you should protect them at all costs. By protecting them, you empower yourself to overcome any obstacles that may come your way or anything that might want to destroy your dreams.

Take the necessary steps to protect your dreams from external factors that could compromise or hinder them. Dream killers must find you ready to face and overcome them so that they won't kill your dreams.

Be careful who you share your dreams with or who you ask to help you make those dreams come true because if you are not careful, others will assist you to destroy them and not achieve them.

Have a character that will help you protect your dreams against any weapon formed against them. Protecting your dreams is essential to achieving the success and happiness you deserve because they will be destroyed if you don't protect them. And you will have regrets and experience the pain of not achieving your dreams.

8. *Believe in your dreams and in yourself to achieve them.*

See yourself achieving your dreams, and let that encourage you whenever you feel discouraged. If you dream of being an inspirational speaker, believe in that dream. See yourself entering a room full of people you want to speak to and delivering your speech at your best.

If you dream of being a business person, believe in your dream and your ability to achieve it. See yourself registering your business, meeting relevant people, and having your business succeed.

Whatever your dream is, believe in it and believe in yourself to achieve it, and nothing will stop you. That will serve as an encouragement every time you get tired or discouraged.

9. *Overcome doubt, discouragement, fear, negative people, and negative thoughts.*

For your dreams to come true, you must overcome doubt, discouragement, fear, negative people, and negative thoughts. Otherwise, they will delay progress in your life and eventually kill your dreams.

Doubt will tell you, *"Not you. You cannot achieve that dream."* Discouragement will say, *"You are tired. You tried, but it is not working. Give up."* Fear will say, *"What if you fail?"*

Negative people will say, *"Stop wasting your time with those crazy and impossible dreams."* Negative thoughts will also give you all the reasons why your dreams will not come true. If you are not careful, you will believe those reasons and give up on your dreams.

Be careful of your everyday conversations with yourself, and replace every negative thought with a positive one. Words are powerful. They can cause you to achieve your dreams or to give up on them. So be careful of how you talk to yourself and about yourself and your dreams. *Be positive and constructive.*

Believe in yourself and your abilities. And never let anyone or anything hold you back. With determination and a positive attitude, you can overcome any obstacle that stands in your way.

Remember that you can achieve great things. Never let negative influences bring you down. But keep pushing forward and stay focused on your dreams, and you will succeed.

10. *Be prepared to avoid missing opportunities*

Preparations meet success. But if you are not prepared, you miss opportunities.

We often have great dreams but fail to prepare ourselves. Unfortunately, we miss out on opportunities when they arise.

Some time ago, I came across a video of a young woman praying for investors to come and invest in her business. She prayed, and God answered her prayers. The investors came and were willing to invest in her business.

The problem was that she prayed but did not prepare. So, upon meeting the investors, she failed to answer some of their questions and convince them why they should invest in her business. It was as if she knew nothing about the business she wanted them to invest in.

Those investors were disappointed and left without investing in her business. She prayed again and asked God why did that happen, and God answered by saying, *"You prayed but did not prepare for your meeting."*

Most of us do this often. We pray for our dreams to come true, but we don't prepare, and because of that, we miss opportunities.

How many opportunities have you missed because you did not prepare for them? How many opportunities will you miss because you are not preparing for them? You expect to meet opportunities for your dreams to come true, so why are you not preparing yourself?

Being unprepared will delay you and cost you lifetime opportunities. I don't think that is something you want to experience. So to avoid that, be prepared. You don't know when you will meet that opportunity you are waiting or hoping for. Let it find you prepared to grab and utilise it.

11. Seek advice and mentorship

King Solomon explains this well in **Proverbs 15:22,** *"Without counsel plans fail, but with many advisers they succeed."*

Simply meaning, as much as we want to do things ourselves, we must accept that *"We need help from others."* The sooner we accept that, the better our lives will be. It will be easy for us to seek advice and mentorship from those who have made it in life.

We need their guidance and encouragement, and we need them to correct us, as they have been there before us. They know the road to success better than we do.

Most of us are not succeeding because we don't want to be mentored or advised. We think less of ourselves when someone advises us or when we have to ask for advice from someone who already made it in life.

We feel like we are nothing or that we know nothing. We forget that *plans fail without counsel, but with many advisers, they succeed.*

One other thing is not having anyone hold you accountable. You have many delays and a lack of commitment. But if you have someone holding you accountable, you know that they will want to see progress. So you are forced to plan and take action so that when you meet again with them, there will be progress.

Whatever career or dream you want to pursue, you need someone who can guide you, share their experience and knowledge with you, and mentor you.

You need someone who can guide you and show you different ways you can apply to achieve your dreams.

Asking for advice and mentorship does not mean you are stupid. It is simply asking someone who has done or achieved what you want to achieve how they did it so that you can also do it. You can learn from them and be the best that you want to be.

They can help you be prepared for the unexpected and remind you that although success can be challenging, it is possible and achievable.

They can give you their tested methods to move from where you are to where you want to be in life. And it also encourages you to believe that *"If they made it, so can you."*

Find a mentor who will help you achieve your dreams and live the life you desire. They have made it and can help you reach the top and succeed in life.

But remember that having a mentor does not mean they do the work for you. It simply means they will guide you, give you tasks, push you to work, and hold you accountable for your progress. *You will still do the work under their supervision.*

Remember, it is important to clearly understand your objectives or what you want to achieve. That way, you would know which mentor you need in your life, as the mentor's job is to help you finish what you started, not to do the job for you.

You can also seek assistance from various sources such as books, articles, and videos. Most people share their journey through some of those sources, and what they share can inspire and guide you to achieve your dreams. Read, listen, research, and equip yourself to achieve your dreams.

12. *Never stop believing in the beauty of your dreams.*

I encourage you to *never give up on your dreams*. And if you have already given up on them, I ask you to dream again. Tell your heart to beat and dream again. Revisit the day you started having your dreams and remember the joy, fulfilment, and contentment you felt.

> *"No matter how apart you think your life has fallen, pick up the pieces and move on. Life goes on."* **- PuleSir**

Remember the life you visualised and were so excited to live and pick up the pieces from there. Look at where it all went wrong. What made you fail or give up on your dreams? What can you do better so that you won't make the same mistake repeatedly?

Take it from there, and live your life one step at a time until you reach your desired destination. *You can and you should because it is possible and achievable.*

Wake up and achieve your dreams

It is time for you to wake up, stand up, and get out there to make things happen in your life. It is time to take action, implement/apply what you have learned, and make sure you achieve your dreams.

It is time to be serious about your dreams, success, and life. Confront your comfort zone, and don't allow it to delay or kill your dreams. Follow dreams that are yours, not other people's dreams, because following other people's dreams can delay or destroy you.

Mix all the ingredients mentioned above, and you will achieve your dreams. You will have the things you want, do what you want to do, be who you want to be, and live the life you desire. *It is in your hands. Make sure you don't disappoint yourself.*

Believe in your dreams and in yourself to achieve them. Believe in the beauty of your dreams and the difference achieving them can make in your life. Believe that you can make your dreams come true.

Stop procrastinating, stop making excuses, and plan and take action to achieve your dreams. Plan and take action to do things you want to do and to have things you want to have so that you can live and enjoy your life to the fullest.

"Never Give Up on your Dreams."

Dreams do come true

If I can dream it, I can live it
If I can see it, I can catch and touch it
If I can love it, I can follow it
If I can dream it, I can be it
Dreams do come true

The future belongs not to everyone,
But to those who, in the beauty of their dreams, believe
Who in themselves trust and believe
Not in luck but in hard work and opportunities
Dreams do come true.

With dreams, the future is bright,
With dreams, success is in your hands
Following them is the right path to choose
With hard work, you make them achievable
Dreams do come true.

Dreams are achievable
With them, you accomplish your mission

The mission to be successful and significant
As success belongs not to everyone
But to those who, in the beauty of their dreams, believe

Dreams are achievable,
If visualised, steps planned, and action taken
Dreams do come true.

About the Author

PuleSir, born **Irish Tshepang Pule,** is an influential, ambitious, and focused person passionate about *"making a difference in other people's lives."* A dedicated youth and community development leader with a mission to *"inspire people to use their gifts, skills, ideas, and creative minds to be successful and significant in life."*

He is an Inspirational Speaker and the Author of **"Beyond Inspiration, and Never Give Up on your Dreams."**

As part of his contribution towards youth and community development in South Africa, he joined the Agape Youth Movement **(AYM)** from 2013 to 2023. He served as the organisation's Content Creator/Manager, Deputy President, Programme Coordinator, and Board Member.

He is a former Radio Presenter at Madibeng FM, Bokone Bophirima FM, and Bojanala FM. Not only did he work as a Presenter, but he was also given the opportunity to work as a Programme Manager, News Reader, Content Producer, Voiceover Artist, and Music Compiler.

The self-proclaimed and well-deserving Agent of Change *is living to make a difference in this world through the gifts and skills God gave him.* With a strong belief in spirituality, motivated by a quote that says: *"With God, nothing shall be impossible."*

A true living Legend.